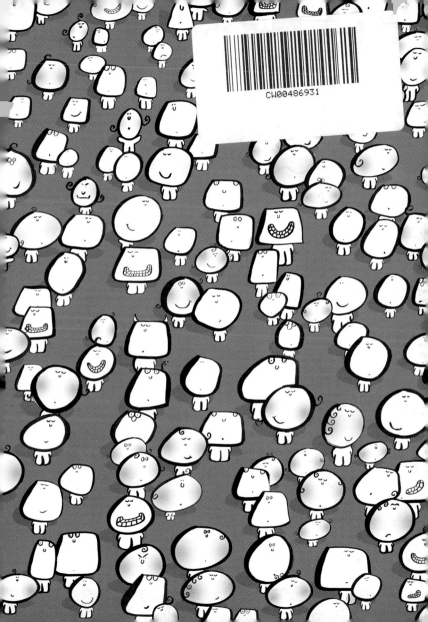

blokehood

with Vimrod

blokehood

beer
is the **oil** that
greases the
engine of
the
soul

vimrod by Lisa Swerling and Ralph Lazar

HarperCollins*Publishers*

my **aim** is to be promoted,
my **goal** is to be boss,
my **aspiration** is
to be powerful,
my **dream** is to be rich,
my **desire** is to be at the top.
but for the moment i'll just
stay here in **bed** for a while

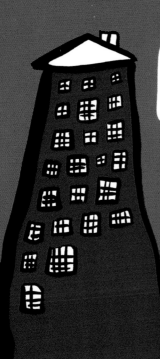

may your **home** always be **too small** to hold all your **friends**, but big enough to hold all your **beers.**

i fart when
provoked

contemporary society is characterised by the watching of football,

punctuated by
brief periods of
industriousness,
warfare and the
mowing of lawns.

i am neither a mr. nor
a dr. nor a prof. nor a sir.
i am a ye grande
olde.

When commuting on a busy train, if you *eat* the finance section of your newspaper as the journey starts, you'll be amazed at how quickly space frees up around you.

burp

now that oil prices are
falling, i reckon the price
of oil will be lower.
i'm not boasting
but i really
understand
the market
OIL
OIL
OIL
OIL
OIL
OIL
OIL
OIL
OIL
OIL
OIL
OIL

deep inside the heart of every man is a philosopher. and inside that philosopher is another, smaller philosopher. inside that one is another really tiny philosopher. and that last philosopher actually couldn't give a shit about philosophy. he loves beer and football and women.

i snore in stereo

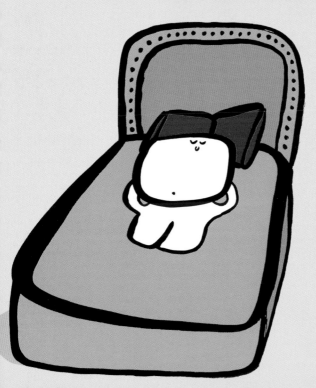

i would like to be a **dog** for a day

so i could pee against my boss' leg without fear of

major repercussions

life is short
and the
unexpected can
suddenly happen.

for instance,
you might be in the
pub with friends and
then suddenly it's
closing time without
you realising it.

i mean how
hectic is
that?

me,

i am in training for the afterlife. apparently once you are there you have to sleep a lot.

i can't come
into the office
today as i am
suffering **FOHP**
(fear of having peaked)

dunno, the words **second** and **helping** just seem to roll off my tongue really well

this is not a bald patch
it's a landing strip for
very small helicopters

there is no place
like **home**.
except the pub.
that is kind of like
home to me.

i can't come into the office today as my head is stuck in a minibar. sorry.

lisa swerling + ralph lazar

are two of the uk's most popular
graphic artists. through their company
last lemon they have brought to life a
range of inspired cartoon characters,
including harold's planet, the brainwaves,
blessthischick and, of course, vimrod.

they are married with two children,
and live in london.

- -

HarperCollins*Publishers*
77–85 Fulham Palace Road, Hammersmith, London W6 8JB

www.harpercollins.co.uk

Published by HarperCollins*Publishers* 2008

1

A catalogue record for this book is available from the British Library

ISBN-10 0 00 726710 X
ISBN-13 978 0 00 726710 1

Set in Bokka
Printed and bound in Italy by Lego SpA

other titles in the Vimrod collection:

drink!
Wine is made to be drunk, I am drunk, therefore am I wine?

shopping
it's the little voices that tell me to go shopping

farting
my farts hospitalise small children

xmas
christmas is coming... run!

dads
life is a journey between the fridge and the sofa

chocolate
life is a struggle between good, evil and chocolate

love
you and me... two hamsters on the spinning-wheel of life

mums
behind every great woman is her bum

life
life is terribly long isn't it? shall we rest?

insults
the way you breathe really irritates

indulgence
girls like us deserve the best, plus a little extra

(watch this space)

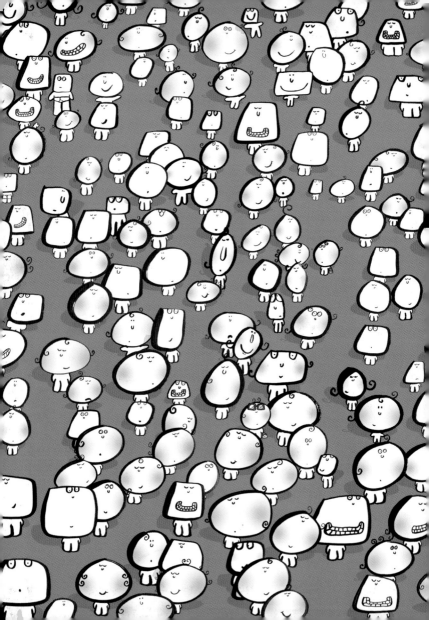